Can I Hit It?

Illustrated by Karen Bell

High-Frequency Words
I   the

Editorial Offices: Glenview, Illinois • Parsippany, New Jersey • New York, New York
Sales Offices: Parsippany, New Jersey • Duluth, Georgia • Glenview, Illinois
Coppell, Texas • Ontario, California

I am Diz.

Can I hit it?

Yes, I can hit it.

I can run.

I can run

in the sun.

Yes, I can win.